D1578000

The Way of the Cross

Fulton J. Sheen

ST PAULS

Nihil Obstat:
Rev. John M. Kuzmich, Censor librorum

Imprimatur:
✠ William E. McManus
Bishop of Fort Wayne, South Bend
May 18, 1982

Bishop Sheen first composed this Way of the Cross for Palm Sunday 1932. It was initially published by the National Council of Catholic Men in 1932 and subsequently by Our Sunday Visitor, Inc. in 1982.

This Alba House edition has been produced by special arrangement with the Estate of Fulton J. Sheen and the Society for the Propagation of the Faith, 366 Fifth Avenue, New York, NY 10001. This edition includes verses from the Stabat Mater taken from *The Prayers of the Pauline Family*.

Produced and designed in the United States of America by the Fathers and Brothers of the Society of St. Paul,
2187 Victory Boulevard, Staten Island, New York 10314-6603,
as part of their communications apostolate.

ISBN: 978-0-8189-0989-4

Printing Information:

Current Printing - first digit	4	5	6	7	8	9	10

Year of Current Printing - first year shown

2017	2018	2019	2020	2021	2022

Dedication

Mary, Mediatrix of all Graces, who
at the foot of the Cross
did bring forth in sorrow
your other children, who we are,
as you did bring forth in joy
your first Child at the crib,
I offer you these prayers
in loving gratitude and hope
that, as our Mother sweet and kind,
you may always be with us
on the Royal Road of the Cross.

Introduction

The author of these meditations on the Way of the Cross has a twofold purpose in offering them in printed form. The first is that they may enkindle in souls a flaming love for the Crucified Christ, who, through His passion and death, revealed to us that it is only through the Cross that we are ever ushered into glory and eternal life.

The second purpose is that those who meditate on the great love of Our Lord for sinners will be kind enough to say a prayer for the author.

Fulton J. Sheen

Prayer Before the Way of the Cross

O Lord Jesus,
the curtain is now about to go up
on the awful and abiding drama
of your redemptive love.
And as I hear your words,
"Take up your cross daily and follow me,"
I stand affrighted, lest its burden
be too great and its shame too bitter.
If I could but see that your command
to follow you to Calvary
was not just an iron law of cruel fate,
but a condition of everlasting happiness,
perhaps I could better make the journey.
But I fear, dear Jesus, that in having you
I must have nothing else besides.
Let my fear be dispelled
in seeing death as the condition of life.
For through your apostle Paul,
you have told us that it is the joy at the end
of the journey that makes us endure my cross.
I shall, then, take up my cross.
O Jesus, why must we love you so!

At the Cross her station keeping,
Stood the mournful Mother weeping,
Close to Jesus to the last.

JESUS CONDEMNED

Jesus Is Condemned to Death

We adore you, O Christ,
and we praise you —
Because by your Holy Cross
you have redeemed the world.

Pilate, the time-serving politician, stepped forward on his sunlit portico. On his right stood Christ, the Just One, who came to give His life for the redemption of many. On his left stood Barabbas, the wicked one, who had incited a revolt and taken a life. Pilate asked the mob to choose between the two: "Whom do you want me to release to you, Barabbas or Jesus?"

How would I have answered that question had I been in the courtyard that Good Friday morning? I cannot escape answering by saying that the question belongs only to the past, for it is as actual now as ever. My conscience is the tribunal of Pilate. Daily, hourly, and every minute of the day, Christ comes before that tribunal, as virtue, honesty, and purity. Barabbas comes as vice, dishonesty, and uncleanness. As often as I choose to speak the uncharitable word, do the dishonest action, or consent to the evil thought, I say in so many words, "Release Barabbas unto me." And to choose Barabbas means to crucify Christ.

Pray for us, O holy Mother of God —
That we may be made worthy
of the promises of Christ.

PRAYER

O Jesus, many times in my life
I have preferred Barabbas to you.
There is no way that I can undo those choices
but to make my way to your feet
and beg your forgiveness.
But that is so humiliating,
for you wear the garment of a fool,
and you bear in your hand
the reed scepter of a mock king!
It is so hard for me to do penance
and to admit that I am guilty!
It is so hard to be seen with you,
who are wearing your crown of thorns.
It is hard! But let me see, Jesus,
that it is harder to wear the crown of thorns.

Through her heart, His sorrow sharing,
All His bitter anguish bearing.
Now at length the sword had passed.

THE CROSS

Jesus Carries His Cross

✝

We adore you, O Christ,
and we praise you —
Because by your Holy Cross
you have redeemed the world.

Our Blessed Lord had been a visitor to our earth but forty days when Simeon, with prophetic vision, declared that this Child would someday become a sign of contradiction. That day had now come, for "He came unto His own, and His own received Him not."

As a symbol of the world's rejection of His life-giving message, His enemies gave Him a Cross, in which one bar is at variance with, or contradicts, the other: the horizontal bar symbolizing death (for all death is flat and prostrate), the vertical bar symbolizing life (for all life is upright and erect).

But by a divine act, Our Lord made the sign of

contradiction the sign of redemption, and converted the Cross into the Crucifix. The Cross is the problem of pain and death; but the Crucifix is the solution. For when the God-man had ennobled it by His presence, He revealed that pain is the condition of pleasure, that death is the prelude to life, and that unless we take up our own crosses and follow Him we cannot be His disciples.

Pray for us, O Holy Mother of God —
That we may be made worthy
of the promises of Christ.

PRAYER

I know, dear Lord, how crosses are made.
Your will is the vertical bar;
my will is the horizontal bar.
When I place my will against your will,
I make a cross.
Up to this point, dear Jesus,
I have done nothing but fashion crosses
by disobeying your holy law
and asserting my own selfish desires.
Grant that I may make you no more crosses,
but henceforth may place the bar of my will
alongside the bar of your will,
and make a yoke that will always be sweet
and a burden that will always be light.

> *O how sad and sore distressed*
> *Was that Mother, highly blessed,*
> *Of the sole-begotten One.*

FIRST FALL

Jesus Falls the First Time

✝

We adore you, O Christ,
and we praise you —
Because by your Holy Cross
you have redeemed the world.

Three times Our Savior was tempted on the mountain, and three times He fell on the way to Mount Calvary. Thus did He atone for our three falls — to the temptations of the flesh, the world, and the devil.

After fasting forty days in the desert, our blessed Lord was hungry. Satan tempted Him first on the part of the flesh, by asking Him to do the natural thing when hungry, namely, to use His power to command that the stones become bread. But the Master rebuked Satan, saying that the food that satisfies the longings of our hearts comes not from the flesh, but from the Spirit of God.

Many times we too have been tempted to give

way to the demands of our lower nature when the spirit should have been served. But unlike our divine Master, we fell by consenting to the promptings of the flesh instead of to the urges of grace, and by doing what is natural when we should have done what is supernatural. And alas! We have found it always true that giving in to selfish impulses has left us hungry, rather than satisfied. On the bread of lower desires, no one can live.

Pray for us, O Holy Mother of God —
That we may be made worthy
of the promises of Christ.

PRAYER

When my bodily frame is buffeted
by the power of Satan,
seal my senses, O Lord,
and keep me mindful that
my body is a temple of the Holy Spirit,
and that only the clean of heart shall see you.
Grant henceforth that by the merits
of this fall under the cross,
I may be saved from the falls of the flesh—
not by bread made from stones,
but by the Bread of Life.

Christ above in torment hangs,
She beneath beholds the pangs
of her dying glorious Son.

MOTHER AND SON

Jesus Meets His Blessed Mother

†

We adore you, O Christ,
and we praise you —
Because by your Holy Cross
you have redeemed the world.

At the marriage feast of Cana, when Mary first noted the embarrassment of the hosts and asked her divine Son to work His first miracle, He answered: "My hour is not yet come." But at her request, He anticipated the hour, and changed water into wine.

His hour, He said, had "not yet come." But *His* hour was *her* hour too, and now it had come! At Cana, He had changed water into wine. On the road to Calvary, the wine is changed into blood. It is the solemn hour of consecration by which she unites herself with the suffering of her beloved Son, to save the world from the terrible embarrassment of sin and from the want of God's redemptive wine of His love. It was the hour in which the world's idea of love was reversed — in which the Son summoned His mother to suffer. Love, then, does not mean "to have"; it means "to be had." It is the giving of oneself for another. No other human being ever loved Jesus as much as Mary did; so we must say that no one else ever suffered for Jesus as Mary did.

Pray for us, O Holy Mother of God —
That we may be made worthy
of the promises of Christ.

PRAYER

Mary, dear Mother,
in this your hour of sorrow,
you are paying dearly for the privilege
of your Immaculate Conception!
Your present sorrows are
the pains of childbirth
by which you are to become
the Mother of Humankind,
just as in Bethlehem
you became the Mother of Jesus,

your First Born.
You are, then,
really my Mother too.
Teach me, Mother, to see
that Jesus calls to suffering
those whom He loves.
And grant that just as Jesus
keeps the best wine of His love
for the hour when we need it most,
so too may He keep you near us
when we need you most —
in all the trials and temptations,
but especially at the hour of our death.

Is there one who would not weep,
Whelmed in miseries so deep,
Christ's dear Mother to behold?

SIMON HELPS

Simon the Cyrenean Helps Jesus to Carry His Cross

†

We adore you, O Christ,
and we praise you —
Because by your Holy Cross
you have redeemed the world.

It was not merely death that sinful people wished our Blessed Savior; it was a particular kind of death upon the sign of contradiction. Fearing that exhaustion and weakness would rob them of unfurling Him, like a banner of warning on top of Mount Calvary, they forced Simon of Cyrene to help Him with His task. Simon saw in the cross only a shameful burden of wood, but not the burden of the world's sins. Hence he became at first an unwilling helper. But a few minutes in the sweet company of Jesus changed his outlook; his slavery became freedom, his constraint became love, and his reluctance became sweet abandon.

We too are like Simon in his first moments; we know about Jesus, but we do not know Jesus. We have feared to be a sharer of His cross, and hence have loved Him little, because we have known Him only a little. We have too often insisted on beginning with pleasure, when it is with pleasure that we should have ended.

Pray for us, O Holy Mother of God —
That we may be made worthy
of the promises of Christ.

PRAYER

Give me, O Jesus,
an understanding of this great mystery:
that it is only at a distance
that the Cross frightens —
that its shadow is really more terrible
than its reality —
that its splinters are more terrifying
than its beams —
that the whole of it is easier to carry
than a part.
You have told us, dear Savior,
that we must each take up our cross daily
and follow in your footsteps.
Grant, then, that when a cross
comes between you and me,
as it did between you and Simon,
I may be willing to follow you as Simon did,
until at last I shall be forevermore
an uncaught captive in your loving hands.

Can the human heart refrain
From partaking in her pain
In that Mother's pain untold?

THE HOLY FACE

Veronica Wipes the Face of Jesus

†

We adore you, O Christ,
and we praise you —
Because by your Holy Cross
you have redeemed the world.

Simon the Cyrenean helped Jesus with His burden. For us, this is a sign that every person is called to the sublime vocation of carrying a cross. On that dread day, Veronica, with a woman's own special vision, looked on a countenance bruised and stained with dust and blood, and saw in it the very Face of Divinity.

Ignoring what others might think, she touched a towel to Jesus' face, and as if to remind us that the likeness between Christ and us is most perfect in suffering and sorrow, the Divine Savior, on His way to Calvary, left the impression of that divinely sorrowful face. By that one act, our Blessed Lord revealed that we can never become like unto Him in the nobility of His birth, when angels sang to the shepherds, not in the glory of His Transfiguration, when His face shone like the sun and His garments were as white as snow. There is only one way we can become exactly like Him, and that is by suffering.

Pray for us, O Holy Mother of God —
That we may be made worthy
of the promises of Christ.

PRAYER

O Lord,
the day I was born anew
of water and the Holy Spirit,
the image of your Cross
was engraved upon my heart.
Today you ask me:
"Whose inscription is written thereon?"
If it be yours, then let me render
to God the things that are God's.
Grant that, like Veronica,
I may brave all human respect
to carry your image about with me,
not on a veil but on the tablet of my heart.
Bestow on me the grace to be so much like you
that others among whom I live
may see something of you in me,
as the maidservant saw something of you in
    Peter.
If they do not see in me the marks of your
    passion,
let them at least see the sparks of your love.

Bruised, derided, cursed, defiled
She beheld her tender Child
All with bloody scourges rent.

SECOND FALL

Jesus Falls the Second Time

We adore you, O Christ,
and we praise you —
Because by your Holy Cross
you have redeemed the world.

In the second temptation, the devil asked our Blessed Lord to abandon Himself wholly to God and to take no care or thought of Himself, saying: "Cast yourself down from the parapet of this Temple, for the angels will bear you up." But the Savior answered: "You shall not tempt the Lord, your God," reminding Satan, and us, that God never saves us against our will, but only when we cooperate with His grace.

The temptation came not from the flesh, but from the world, which so many times has said to us: "Cast yourself down on the rocks of sin; abandon yourself to God; God is merciful; He will bear you up; there is plenty of time for repentance — God will take care of you." And many times we, unlike the Master, have given in to such whisperings. We have sinned by presumption, then made a halfhearted resolution to amend our lives — and then we sinned again.

Pray for us, O Holy Mother of God —
That we may be made worthy
of the promises of Christ.

Dear Savior,
by this, your second fall,
you atoned for my excessive love of the world
and for the many times I abused your mercy
and goodness as an excuse for sinning again.
By lifting yourself up again,
you have merited for me the grace
to lift myself up once more
and continuing the journey
with you to Calvary.
Free me from the spirit of the world.
Let me see that it profits me nothing
to gain the whole world
and lose my immortal soul.
You have told me that the world will hate me
if I love you.
So when the world scorns me most,
I ask that I may be consoled by the memory
that it has hated you before it hated me.

For the sins of His own nation
She saw Him hang in desolation
Till His spirit forth He sent.

THE HOLY WOMEN

Jesus Comforts the Women of Jerusalem

We adore you, O Christ,
and we praise you —
Because by your Holy Cross
you have redeemed the world.

Of all things on earth, that which we know least is ourselves. We know the sins and the defects of others a thousand times better than we know our own; and we see immediately the mote in our neighbor's eye, but not the beam in our own eyes. That great truth was illuminated on the way to Calvary. The pious women of Jerusalem, though quite unafraid to show their piety before impious men, saw only the suffering Jesus whom they loved; they did not see the loving Christ who suffered for them. They sympathized with His pain, but they did not see themselves as the cause of that pain. It was their sins — and ours as well — which

He took upon Himself. And as if to bring that truth home to us all, there welled up from the depths of His sacred heart these words: "Weep not for me, but weep for yourselves."

Pray for us, O holy Mother of God —
That we may be made worthy
of the promises of Christ.

PRAYER

O Jesus,
let me see the connection
between my sins and your Calvary.
Let me not weep for you apart from me,
but for you on account of me.
Let me see that if I had been less proud,
the crown of thorns would have been less
      piercing;
that if I had been less selfish,
the cross would have been less heavy;
that if I had been less sinful,
the road to Calvary would have been shorter.
Give me the grace to weep for my sins.
And may my fountain of tears become,
through the example of your love,
a fountain of everlasting joy.

O my Mother, fount of love,
Touch my spirit from above;
Make my heart with yours accord.

THIRD FALL

Jesus Falls the Third Time

✝

We adore you, O Christ,
and we praise you —
Because by your Holy Cross
you have redeemed the world.

The third temptation on the mount was not temptation by the flesh or by the world, but by the devil himself. Satan asked our Blessed Lord to fall down and adore him, promising to give Him all of earth's kingdoms. But Jesus said to him, "The Lord your God shall you adore, and Him alone shall you serve."

There have been countless occasions in our lives when we have exchanged the priceless treasure of divine grace for some passing toy or pleasure. Unlike Christ, we have believed the devil's lies and traded away eternity for time, peace for remorse, and our freedom as children of God for the terrible slavery of sin. And each time we have learned that whereas Satan promises a kingdom of pleasure, he actually gives only a wasteland of unhappiness and pain.

Pray for us, O holy Mother of God —
That we may be made worthy
of the promises of Christ.

PRAYER

Many times, dear Jesus, I promised you,
after having fallen to temptation
by the flesh and the world,
that I would never fall again.
Your third fall, dear Jesus,
is a witness that I have fallen
by the snares of the devil.
But by rising again,
you have given me another reason to hope.
You have taught me that there are
two kinds of person I can be:
a person who falls down and stays down,
or a person who falls but gets up again.
By this, your third fall,
you purchased for me the grace
of rising again each time I fall.
The devil would give up the world
to make me his own.
You gave up your very life
to keep me for yourself,
to show me that I am worth saving.

Make me feel as you have felt,
Make my soul to glow and melt
With the love of Christ my Lord.

THE STRIPPING

Jesus Is Stripped of His Garments

†

We adore you, O Christ,
and we praise you —
Because by your Holy Cross
you have redeemed the world.

God's dealing with humanity has been a continuous process kept in motion by His overflowing goodness. The first overflowing was in giving things existence, and that was Creation. The second overflowing was in His telling us the secret of His love for us, and that was Revelation. Finally, this love that has no limits resulted in the Incarnation. As Saint Paul wrote, God "emptied Himself," cast His glory into the background, and took upon Himself the human form and habit of man.

Now, on the hill called Calvary, Jesus willed not only to empty Himself of His divine glory, but to abandon His claim to any earthly possessions. He, the Heavenly Vagabond who had nowhere to lay His head, was stripped of His garments, so that in death He might have nothing, but give all.

Pray for us, O holy Mother of God —
That we may be made worthy
of the promises of Christ.

Prayer

Jesus my Savior,
if you emptied yourself
so that I could have divine life,
did you not intend that I should be filled with it?
Grant, then, dear Jesus,
that I may empty myself of selfishness
so that I may be filled with your selflessness;
grant that I may empty myself of sin,
and be filled with your graces;
and grant that I may empty myself of
    earthliness,
and be filled with heavenliness.
Strip from me the garments of worldliness,
and clothe me in the white robe of baptism.
Through poverty in earthly things,
I can become rich in spirit.
Strengthen me so that I may welcome sacrifice
and accept bodily suffering as my way
of repaying you for, and joining you in,
the merit of your Passion.

Holy Mother pierce me through
In my heart each wound renew
Of my Savior crucified.

THE NAILING

Jesus Is Nailed to the Cross

✝

*We adore you, O Christ,
and we praise you —
Because by your Holy Cross
you have redeemed the world.*

Our Blessed Lord mounts His pulpit for the last time. This time, it is not Peter's boat or the Galilean hills, but the pulpit of the cross. Like the words He shall utter from it, this pulpit will itself be eloquent even when time shall end. The Preacher is the living Word of God; the congregation is made up of soldiers who play at dice for His seamless garment, of unbelievers whose mouths are trumpets of hate and blasphemy, and of three faithful ones — Mary, Magdalene, and John. Those three faithful ones are the three types of souls always to be found beneath the cross; they represent innocence, penitence, and priesthood. The last words of Jesus are spoken first on behalf of the mockers and blasphemers: "Forgive them, for they know not what they do." Next, to sinners: "This day you shall be with me in paradise." And finally, to saints: "Mother, behold your son."

Pray for us, O holy Mother of God —
That we may be made worthy
of the promises of Christ.

PRAYER

Dear Jesus,
the words you spoke from the cross
reveal your tremendous thirst
for the salvation of all your human creatures.
From your example
I begin to see what love really is,
and to become aware
of how often I have crucified love.
Your hands, raised to bless me,
I have nailed fast.
Your feet, which have sought me
when I was caught in the snares of sin,
I pierced with an iron stake.

Your lips, which have so often called me
from the paths of wickedness,
I have blistered with dust.
Your words of forgiveness
I only now begin to hear.
And I begin to understand that
when I pierced your heart,
it was my own that I was slaying.
So now I return to the cross,
the chalice of all miseries,
the hope of nearly hopeless sinners.
I stand beneath your cross, O Lord,
so that I can learn that
it takes little time to become a saint,
but much love.
And I understand now,
that if I had never sinned,
I could never call you "Savior."

Let me share with you His pain,
Who for all my sins was slain,
Who for me in torment died.

JESUS DIES

Jesus Dies Upon the Cross

We adore you, O Christ,
and we praise you —
Because by your Holy Cross
you have redeemed the world.

The great funeral pyre of suffering gradually burns itself out, and the blood of the God-man dries on the wood of the cross, as a sign of His passing. His garments are consigned to His executioners, His blood to the earth, His body to the grave, His mother to John, and His soul to His Heavenly Father. Having finished the last word of His testament, He bows His head and dies. His spirit descends into Limbo, and His escort there is a thief. All is finished now. God has had His revenge on Satan and sin.

Three things cooperated in the fall of the human race from grace: the disobedient man, Adam; the proud woman, Eve; and the tree. To restore that grace to us, God relied on the obedient man, Christ; the humble woman, Mary; and the tree of the cross. But at the moment of Christ's death, His triumph was still hidden from human eyes. A mocking voice cried out, "Others He saved. Himself He cannot save."

Pray for us, O holy Mother of God —
That we may be made worthy
of the promises of Christ.

PRAYER

O Jesus,
how truly you have taught us:
no man can save himself if he is to save another.
Your weakness in the face of death was
      but a sign
of the obedience that the law of sacrifice requires.
The leaves on a tree cannot save themselves
if they are to bud the stems and branches
      by their fall.
The acorn cannot save itself if it is to
      become the oak.
And so it seems, dear Jesus,
that you could not save yourself from death
if you were to save us from sin.
May I have an everlasting love
for the redemption you have won for me.
And may I always remember that
by accepting my own cross in this life,
I will — oh, strangest of paradoxes —
save my life for eternity.

Let me mingle tears with you,
Mourning Him who mourned for me,
All the days that I may live.

THE DESCENT

Jesus Is Lowered from the Cross

We adore you, O Christ,
and we praise you —
Because by your Holy Cross
you have redeemed the world.

More than thirty years earlier, Jesus had left His Father's heavenly home and traveled to this world. We may think of Him as God's Prodigal Son, who went off to a foreign country and spent Himself for the good of the people of that country. He opened their blind eyes to God's light, and He opened their ears to the words of the gospel. Finally, on a small mound of earth called Calvary, He gave away the substance of His body and blood on behalf of that sinful people.

Taken down from the cross of execution, His body was placed in the arms of His mother, who still recalled the first time she held Him in her arms at Bethlehem. Is it possible that she recalled also that the pierced hands of Jesus had once been warmed by the breath of oxen? Is it possible that her eyes filled with new tears as she remembered that she had once nourished His body with food from her own?

Pray for us, O Holy Mother of God —
That we may be made worthy
of the promises of Christ.

Prayer

Yes, Mary, this is not Bethlehem, but
      Calvary.
Those hands that once accepted
the gifts of the Magi
have now been pierced with rude nails.
That brow on which divine majesty made
      its throne
is now wearing a crown of piercing thorns.
Those infant feet that were once too small
to bear the weight of divine omnipotence
are now again unable to walk.
Between Bethlehem and Calvary, dear Mary,
lies the chasm of sin.
Be my intercessor at the throne of justice
      and mercy,
O Mother of Sorrows and Help of Sinners.
I come now to you, Mary
as a repentant prodigal,
wishing to draw from your heart
the seven swords.

By the cross with you to stay,
There with you to weep and pray,
Is all I ask of you to give.

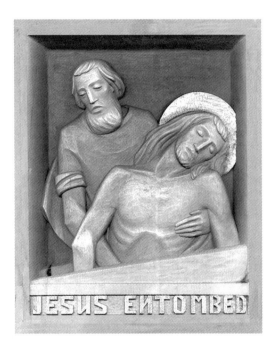

JESUS ENTOMBED

Jesus Is Laid in the Tomb

✝

We adore you, O Christ,
and we praise you —
Because by your Holy Cross
you have redeemed the world.

The world showed little hospitality to our Blessed Lord, who is Master of life and death. For His birth, there was available only a rough-and-ready shelter for animals. For death, He was given the hard bed of the cross, with a crown of thorns as a pillow; and His hands and feet were tucked into that bed with nails. The glory of His birth was hidden in the least of the cities of Israel. The meaning of His death was hidden from human eyes in the greatest city of this world. Born in a stranger's cave, buried in a stranger's grave: thus did Christ teach us that human birth and human death were equally foreign to Him. For those things are foreign to God.

> *Pray for us, O holy Mother of God —*
> *That we may be made worthy*
> *of the promises of Christ.*

PRAYER

Sweet Jesus,
now I understand —
as your lifeless body is placed
in the tomb of a stranger —
that the law of life is also the law of death;
that everything that lives must also die;
and that nothing dies without something coming
to life.
You have shown me, by your life,
that unless there is a cross,
there can be no empty tomb;
that unless there is a crown of thorns,
there can be no heavenly crown;
and that unless the body be scourged,
it can never be glorified.
With the joy of your resurrection before me,

I ask for the strength to endure my cross
and to share in your suffering,
until that next resurrection day,
when, in the heavenly Jerusalem,
all tears shall be wiped away.
I pray also, O Lord,
for all whom this world rejects,
and to whom it denies any hospitality.
Welcome them, loving Savior,
into your kingdom,
where you reign forever and ever. Amen.

While my body here decays,
May my soul your goodness praise,
Safe in Paradise with you. Amen.

Prayer After the Way of the Cross

Dear Jesus,
you are the living Word of God.
You have told us that the Word of God
is a seed that brings forth life
only if it falls to the ground.
You are the seed of everlasting life,
and you fell to the earth by your death
on that first Good Friday.
But you rose to glorious life
on that first Easter Sunday.
You have taught us that Christian living
is actually a dying to this world
in this Calvary of time,
and that this life is but a prelude
to the eternity-long Easter
that awaits us in your heavenly kingdom.
Grant that on the last day,
when you come again in glory
upon the clouds of heaven
to judge the living and the dead,
bearing your cross as the sign

of your triumph over sin and death,
I may be able to show you my cross
and hear you say: "Come,
you blessed of my Father,
into the kingdom prepared for you
from all eternity." Amen.

Our Father
Hail Mary
Glory Be to the Father

Those who devoutly pray the Stations of the Cross may obtain
a plenary indulgence if they also receive Holy Communion
and offer prayers for the Pope's intention within several days
beforehand or afterward.